Contents

About this book

How do you wrestle an alligator? Send morse code signals? Escape from a burning building? Treat an insect sting? Identify animals from their tracks? Fend off a mountain lion? Survive on a desert island? If you've ever wondered how to do any of these things, then read on. This book contains information, help, and advice on just about everything you will ever need to know in a survival situation.

COLOUR-CODED SECTIONS

To make things simple, this book has been divided into six colour-coded categories. Each category gives important information about what to do in different situations.

HOW TO SURVIVE IN THE WILDERNESS

FINDING YOUR WAY IN THE WILDERNESS

ENCOUNTERS WITH DANGEROUS ANIMALS

SURVIVING THE ELEMENTS

FIRST AID

URBAN SURVIVAL

EXTRA INFORMATION

Every page has lots of useful hints and tips. Whenever an activity might be dangerous, we have added a star to remind you to get adult help.

A TRIAL RUN

Hopefully, you will never need to actually use any of the survival methods described in this book. But it may make you feel more confident just knowing you could cope in any circumstance. If you do want to try out any of these methods, always ask an adult to help you, and carefully follow all the safety precautions. But remember, just to be on the safe side, leave stuff like lighting fires, obtaining water from plants, and wrestling fierce animals to grown-ups!

JUST A THOUGHT

It is always a good idea to learn as much as you can about different emergency situations, so why don't you do some extra homework?

For example, you could read up on poisonous plants found in your area, or do a bit of research to see which dangerous animals, snakes, and insects live near your home. You could also check to see if your school or local authority holds first aid and survival courses for young people.

Packing your backpack

Packing the right things in your backpack is extremely important. Consider your situation and take only the bare essentials. There is not much point taking a hair dryer if you cannot plug it in, is there! So DO NOT carry useless weight that will slow you down. If you are travelling by car, pack extra supplies such as a portable stove, tools, toiletries and extra food, water, and clothes. There might even be enough room to take a few books or games.

Pack several thin, loose layers of clothing rather than one thick jumper. Layers of clothes will help to keep you warm in cold climates and cool in the heat. Thick, bulky clothes will only restrict your movements and are more difficult to dry. Light, quick-drying cotton trousers and a "breathable" hooded jacket will also help to protect you against wind and rain.

* Pack at least one complete change of clothing.

* Save space by loosely rolling up all clothing.

* Wear comfortable walking boots.

* A hat has two uses: in cold conditions it helps to keep in your body heat, and in hot conditions, it protects you from the sun.

Essential Gear

Waterproof wash bag

Shampoo

Towel

Toothbrush and paste

Soap

Flannel

Toilet tissue

Sleeping bag

Tent

Sleeping mat

Tent poles

Ground sheet

Water bottle

Cooking pot with a lid

Plastic mug and plate

Knife, fork, and spoon

Can opener

High energy foods (such
as beans, nuts, dried
fruit, malt bread)

PACKING TIPS

To save space, stuff
socks inside shoes, pack
small items into empty
corners, and loosely roll
shorts and t-shirts. Put
your toiletries in a zip
lock bag, just in case
they leak.

Things to remember

* Use a thick, waterproof bag to line your backpack, so everything inside stays dry.

* Put the heaviest things at the top of your backpack, so you carry the weight across your shoulders.

* Things you need to find quickly, like sun block, should go in the side pockets.

YOUR SURVIVAL GEAR

Keep these vital items in a waterproof container that fits inside your backpack.

Compass ✷ Whistle ✷ Candles ✷ Small mirror (to send signals) ✷ Waterproof pen ✷ Matches ✷ Penknife ✷ Needle and thread ✷ Emergency money ✷ First aid kit ✷ String and rope (to make equipment) ✷ Torch (and batteries)

Always pack and wear sunblock when you are outside for a long time.

7

Building a shelter

Whether you camp in a tent or a homemade shelter, it should protect you from the cold, wind, snow, sun, and rain. Look for flat, slightly raised ground, in a sheltered position. Avoid valleys and deep hollows, as they can become wet and frosty at night. Shelters built on hilltops are at risk from wind, driving rain, and cold. Never build a shelter near a site that is prone to flash floods, mudslides, or in an avalanche area.

You will need

Thick sheet of plastic,
2 m x 4 m
(6.5 ft x 13 ft)
Six large, heavy stones
Small, round pebbles
Six lengths of cord
Two twigs or sticks
Penknife

HOW TO DO IT

If you do not have a tent, you can make this simple shelter.

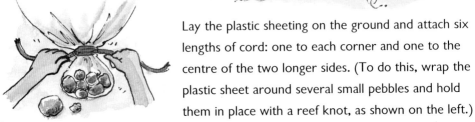

Lay the plastic sheeting on the ground and attach six lengths of cord: one to each corner and one to the centre of the two longer sides. (To do this, wrap the plastic sheet around several small pebbles and hold them in place with a reef knot, as shown on the left.)

To hold the sheet down, wrap the loose end of each cord around a large, heavy stone. Tie half-hitch knots in the wrapped cords to secure them to the stones.

Using a penknife, carve one end of each stick so it is rounded and carve the other end to a point. Slot the sticks into each end of the folded sheet and firmly push the pointed ends into the ground. Adjust the stones to make the sheet a taught, triangular shape.

Do not lean things against the sides of your shelter; it will cause water to seep in when it rains.

KNOTTY PROBLEM

1 To make a *reef knot*, take two pieces of rope and bring the right piece (green here) over and under the left piece (yellow here).

2 Bring the green piece over the yellow piece.

3 Tuck the green piece under the yellow piece.

4 Pull on both ropes to secure the knot.

5 Undo the knot by pushing the two ends of rope towards each other.

1 To make a *half-hitch knot*, first make a loop.

2 Bring the right-hand end of the rope through the back of the loop and out to the front.

3 Pull both ends tight to secure the knot.

Making a fire

A fire has many different uses: it keeps you warm, boils water, cooks food, and dries your clothes. It can even be used for signalling! So it is important for you to know how to make and light a fire in all kinds of conditions. You are cold, wet, miserable... and stranded! So what do you do? Well, the good news is that you have a box of matches... but you will still need three other ingredients – tinder, kindling, and fuel – to make a fire.

Always ask for adult help before attempting to build and light a fire.

Tinder is the most important part of a fire, as a fire cannot be started by directly lighting thick sticks. You can use any dry material like shredded bark, straw and grasses, wood shavings, steel wool, charred cloth, paper, or foam rubber as tinder.

Kindling is a little larger than tinder. Coniferous seed cones and needles, small, dry twigs, or wood doused with flammable materials can be used as kindling. Lay them around the tinder.

Finally, you will need fuel. Dead wood, the insides of fallen trees and branches, twisted bunches of grass, peat, or moss, dead cactus, and dried animal dung all work if dry.

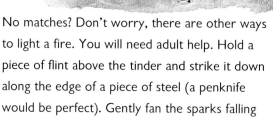

No matches? Don't worry, there are other ways to light a fire. You will need adult help. Hold a piece of flint above the tinder and strike it down along the edge of a piece of steel (a penknife would be perfect). Gently fan the sparks falling onto the tinder to produce a flame.

FIRE SAFETY

Before lighting a fire, there are some important safety rules to remember and follow.

Keep a bucket of water nearby, in case your fire spreads. ✳ **Choose a sheltered site.** ✳ Light your fire in a trench if there are strong winds. ✳ **Light your fire well away from trees, bushes, and wooden fences.**

Things to remember

✳ Always ask permission before lighting a fire.

✳ With adult help, cut and remove a square of turf; light your fire on the soil beneath.

✳ When you have finished with your fire, replace the square of turf.

✳ Flint is a kind of stone found in the ground. You can buy it in camping stores.

Tasty camp food

You can cook food over an open fire in several ways. But before you begin, wait for the flames to die down, leaving just the glowing embers. The easiest way is to use skewers. Thread cubes of food onto skewers pre-soaked in water, and hold them over the embers until they are cooked. This works well for snacks, but if you are making a feast for all your friends, a tripod or grill is the ideal cooking tool.

To make a tripod, tie three 1 m (3 ft) fairly straight branches together with string and secure them with a reef knot (see page 9). Spread out the sticks to form a tripod. You can hang a cooking pot from string tied to a strong twig and fastened to a tripod.

To make a simple grill, tie three sticks to the tripod base. Next, lay smaller sticks, close together, on top to form the grill. Try to find green sticks, as the moisture they contain will ensure they do not burn easily.

For the ultimate snack, thread marshmallows onto thin sticks. Hold them over a campfire until they turn brown. Eat them straight away... yum, yum!

For a more substantial meal, thread alternate pieces of meat and vegetables onto a soaked skewer. Brush with oil, then rest the skewer on top of your grill.

Always make sure meat is cooked thoroughly before you eat it; there should be no blood when you pierce it.

TASTY SOUP

To make a tasty and nourishing soup, put cubes of meat and vegetables into your cooking pot with water and stock cubes. Leave them to simmer over your campfire for at least one hour. If you do not have any meat or stock cubes, add herbs instead.

Things to remember

* Nuts and dried fruit are an ideal high-energy snack that will fit neatly in your pocket.

* Never re-heat meat you have cooked over a camp fire.

* Carefully wrap, and dispose of, any left-over food, otherwise animals will be attracted to your camp.

Water for survival

A human can survive for three weeks without food, but only three days without water. So, always conserve what you have and do not wait until you run out of water before looking for fresh supplies. You need to drink at least 2.5 litres (0.5 gallons) of water a day. But, you will need more water if you suffer from extreme heat or cold exposure, high altitude exposure, vomiting, diarrhoea, or burns, and after exercise.

Safe drinking water can be found in many different places, so always look for the signs. Some water sources are more difficult to find than others, but if you watch the behaviour of birds, bees, and flies, they will lead you to water.

Lots of green vegetation often means the plants are drinking from water near the surface. Swarming insects, especially bees and columns of ants, are often seen near water. Most flies keep within 90 metres (100 yards) of water near the surface.

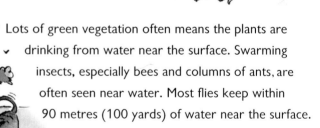

Grazing animals and grain-eating birds are often not far from water. They drink at dawn and dusk.

You can get water by melting snow and ice. Hang a fabric bag full of ice or snow near a fire and collect the water droplets in a container. Ice produces twice as much water as snow for half the heat.

Always boil ice before drinking it and avoid sea ice.

Early risers can also collect morning dew by placing a clean cloth on the grass and then wringing out the water into a container.

WATER FROM PLANTS

Some vines and other plants contain a nutritious liquid. Cut the flower stalk and drain the fluid into a container.

Plants with edible drinking water include sweet acacia, colocynth, agave, saxual, rattan palm, cactus, and grape. ✳ Plants with edible sap include palm, sago palm, fishtail palm, sugar palm, and buri palm.

How to avoid dehydration

* Rest, do not talk. Breathe through your nose, not your mouth.

* Do not lie on hot or heated surfaces.

* Stay in the shade and try to keep cool.

* Eat as little as possible; your body uses water to digest food.

Safe water

It is not enough to just find a water source. You will also need to collect, store, and keep it clean. There are lots of ways to do these things, but they are time-consuming, so a clever camper will always pitch camp near a water tap! That way, you can fill up large, clean bottles of water and keep the water fresh and cool in the shade. But, if you are stranded in the middle of nowhere, you will need to try the following methods.

Wrap a cloth around a healthy, slanted tree and make sure that the bottom of the cloth drips into a clean container. Now sit and wait.

Cacti also contain lots of water. But be careful, as some cacti are poisonous. Cacti that provide good, safe water are Prickly pears, Barrel cacti, and Saquarro cacti.

Only drink clear liquid that is not bitter and does not burn your tongue. Always carry out a taste test to ensure the water is safe (see page 19).

Finally, you can place a large, clean plastic bag over a healthy, leafy tree branch or large shrub. Seal the bag at the branch. Weight the branch so that condensation from the leaves flows into the bag. Use a new branch every day and collect your water at the end of each day.

Water sources that are unsafe

* Lakes in deserts: they often have no outlets and are salt lakes.

* Any water source that does not have green vegetation around it.

* Water that is discoloured.

* Any water that has a strong odour, or has foam or bubbles in it.

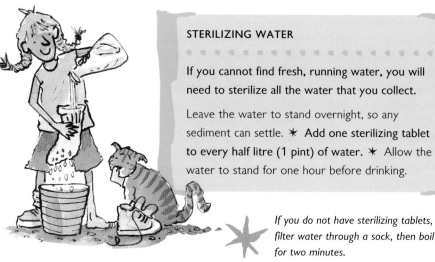

STERILIZING WATER

If you cannot find fresh, running water, you will need to sterilize all the water that you collect.

Leave the water to stand overnight, so any sediment can settle. * Add one sterilizing tablet to every half litre (1 pint) of water. * Allow the water to stand for one hour before drinking.

If you do not have sterilizing tablets, filter water through a sock, then boil it for two minutes.

17

Hunter gatherers

Plants, fruits, and berries contain good sources of protein, carbohydrates, vitamins, and minerals. A few plants even contain fat. All plants provide fibre. Some plants are poisonous, so only eat ones you recognize and know are edible. If, however, you are ship-wrecked on a desert island with no hope of rescue, and you do not recognize any plants around you, do a taste test before trying anything new.

Salt is essential for human survival, and you need a daily intake of 10 g (0.5 oz).

Unless you know what it is, never eat any of the following:

* Red plants and bulbs.
* Plants with umbrella-shaped flowers or a milky sap. Plants that irritate or burn the skin.
* White and yellow berries, as they are poisonous.
* Finally, be careful with red berries; half of them are poisonous, too.

Deadly fungi do not taste unpleasant and symptoms of poisoning may not appear for several hours. So any fungi should be avoided at all costs.

Plants growing in water or moist soil are usually safe to eat. The inner bark of a tree may be eaten raw, but avoid the outer bark. All cereal grain and other grasses can be ground up and mixed with water. Most nuts can be eaten raw. Edible flowers include wild rose, papaya, banana, and horseradish.

TASTE TEST

To find out if a plant is safe to eat, carefully follow these steps.

Put a piece of the plant on the inside of your elbow for 15 minutes. ✶ If there is no reaction, put it on the outer surface of your lip to test for burning or itching. ✶ If there is no reaction after three minutes, hold it on your tongue for 15 minutes. ✶ No reaction? Chew a piece and hold it in your mouth for 15 minutes. Do not swallow! ✶ Still OK? Swallow the food. ✶ Wait eight hours. If any ill effects occur, make yourself sick and drink lots of water. ✶ Feel fine? Eat half a cup of the plant. Wait eight hours. If you still feel okay, the plant is safe to eat.

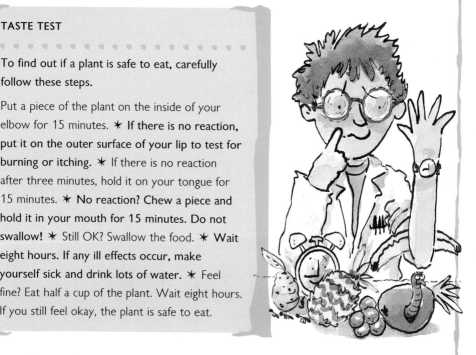

Things to remember

✶ Do not eat for eight hours before starting a taste test.

✶ Discard plants with strong or acid odours.

✶ Test one part of the plant at a time.

Sending signals

If you are lost or stranded, it is vital you can send signals that a rescue team will be able to see clearly. Almost any signal repeated three times is recognized as a distress signal, such as fires, columns of smoke, or flashes of light. If you are using noises or lights, wait one minute between each group of three. There are many ways to send a signal, depending on the materials available and the terrain.

To signal at night, build a fire that gives out a lot of light. A burning tree is a good way to attract attention, providing it is clear of other trees.

In daylight, smoke can be seen over long distances. Signal fires should be built, covered, and maintained ready to be lit at short notice. Burning green leaves, moss, or damp wood produces white smoke. Rubber or oil-soaked rags produce black smoke.

If you need to send a ground to air signal, make the signal as large as possible. It needs to be clearly visible from the air, be in proportion, and stand out against the surrounding area.

Morse signals are sent by flashing lights on and off, or waving a brightly coloured rag on a stick, or by a heliograph (using the sun and a reflector).

To send heliograph signals, use the sun and a reflector to flash light (mirrors are best). Never signal by heliograph to an aircraft except in a survival situation.

For rag signals, move your stick for dashes and for dots. Keep dash pauses slightly longer than dot movements.

USEFUL WORDS TO REMEMBER IN MORSE

When sending morse messages by flashing a light, timing is important. Long flashes are dashes and quick flashes are dots.

SOS
● ● ● | — — — | ● ● ●

SEND
● ● ● | ● | — ● | — ● ●

DOCTOR
— ● ● | — — — | — ● — ● | — | — — — | ● ● — ●

HELP
● ● ● ● | ● | ● — ● ● | ● — — ●

INJURY
● ● | — ● | ● — — — | ● ● — | ● — ● | — ● — —

TRAPPED
— | ● — ● | ● — | ● — — ● | ● — — ● | ● | — ● ●

LOST
● — ● ● | — — — | ● ● ● | —

WATER
● — — | ● — | — | ● | ● — ●

Tracks and trails

Footprints and excrement will tell you almost everything you need to know about an animal. Footprints show what kind of animal it is, and in which direction it is moving. The size and depth of a footprint also indicates the animal's size. The temperature of excrement tells you how fresh it is and how long ago the animal was in the area. Excrement and food remains also tell you if the animal is a meat or plant eater.

If you check out any animal excrement, make sure you wash your hands very thoroughly afterwards.

Following animal tracks in the desert is quite tricky, as the wind will blow the tracks away very quickly. You are better off looking for their excrement instead. You can tell how fresh the excrement is by how moist it is. The less moisture, the older it is.

Tracking jungle animals is another tough one. Because of the thick vegetation, footprints are hard to find, so your sense of hearing and smell are really useful. Look for the remains of fruit, nuts, and any disturbance, as these signs will put you on an animal's trail.

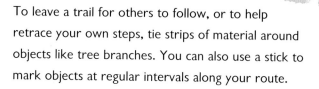

Animal noises can tell you a lot, too. The sound tells you what kind of animal it is – and where it is! After all, there is nothing worse than a gorilla jumping on your back just as you are going to eat your lunch!

To leave a trail for others to follow, or to help retrace your own steps, tie strips of material around objects like tree branches. You can also use a stick to mark objects at regular intervals along your route.

COVERING YOUR TRACKS

To disguise your tracks from other people, do not walk on muddy earth and use twigs to brush away your footprints. This will mean walking backwards... so make sure you do not walk into a tree, or walk into a big hungry animal who is ready for some breakfast!

Things to remember

* Big, heavy animals will leave deep footprints. Small, light animals will leave shallow prints.

* When laying a trail, place markers at the side of your path, so they are less likely to be disturbed.

* If you need to escape from a hungry animal, cross water to shake off your scent.

Finding your way

A **compass is** one of the most important pieces of survival equipment. It will help you to navigate, or find your way. It takes time to learn the basics, so use a compass at home before you venture into the wilderness. If you do not have a compass, you can make your own with a magnet and sewing needle. You can also work out where north, east, south, and west are by just using the sun!

Compasses contain magnets, so do not put them near metal objects.

The numbers around the compass dial are like the degrees in a circle. North is at 0°, east is at 90°, south is at 180°, and west is at 270°. To find the exact direction of an object or place, you need to take its bearing. Rest your compass on a flat surface.

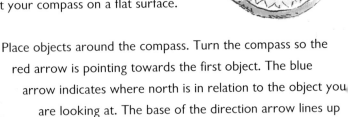

Place objects around the compass. Turn the compass so the red arrow is pointing towards the first object. The blue arrow indicates where north is in relation to the object you are looking at. The base of the direction arrow lines up with a number on the compass dial – the bearing.

Make a sundial to use the sun to find directions. Early in the morning, push a stick into the ground. Mark the end of its shadow with a stone. As the sun moves from east to west, its shadow will move, too.

A magnetized needle works just like a compass, swinging around to point to magnetic north.

Through the day, mark the tip of the sun's shadow with stones. The stones will form an arc. Draw a straight line between the stones, this is your east-west line. Face east, north will be on your left. South is opposite north.

MAKE YOUR OWN COMPASS

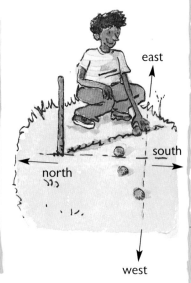

With the eye of a sewing needle pointing down, stroke a magnet downwards along the length of the needle. This will magnetize the needle. ✳ Push the point of the needle through a sliced cork. ✳ Draw an arrow on the cork towards the point of the needle. This is your north point. Draw letters to indicate east, south, and west. ✳ Half-fill a bowl with water, rest it on a flat surface and float the cork in it. ✳ When the water has settled, the needle will point north.

Things to remember

✳ The sun rises in the east and sets in the west.

✳ In the Northern Hemisphere, the sun will be due south at noon. In the Southern Hemisphere, it will be due north at noon.

The Countryside Code

Follow the Countryside Code whenever you are outdoors, to ensure the countryside is a place that everyone can enjoy. Always think about the safety of wild animals, plants, and other people. Make sure you have permission to enter a field and always stick to the footpath. If there is not a footpath, walk around the outside. No matter how pretty they are, never pick flowers or pull up plants.

If you are walking at night, wear light-coloured clothes so that you can be seen easily. Always face traffic on your side of the road. This way, drivers will see you more easily, and you will see them! Wearing fluorescent bands or reflectors will help to make sure you are clearly visible at night.

Always collect your litter before leaving a spot and take it home with you. Remember that litter-filled rivers, ponds, and fields endanger the lives of wild animals, fish, and plants.

Do not assume that it is safe to walk through a field. There may be crops growing that can be damaged by your big stomping feet, or you might find yourself face-to-face with a wild animal!

Animals are very protective of their young and their territory. They are likely to attack if they feel threatened. Even a fluffy, sweet-looking sheep will charge at you if it feels threatened.

PEACE AND QUIET

The countryside is a place to reflect quietly, enjoy the scenery, and to listen to the gentle bird songs around you. It is not a place to play your latest heavy metal or rock CD full blast! You might enjoy the music, but other people and animals will not, that's for sure!

Things to remember

* Even small fires can get out of control, so be careful where you light one. (See page 10.)

* Close gates behind you to ensure that animals cannot escape from their fields.

* Keep your dog on a lead when walking through fields to ensure it does not scare animals or damage crops.

Bulls, bears, and lions

Sheep, ducks, and donkeys are one thing, but what do you do if faced by a raging bull, a wild bear, or a mountain lion? Sometimes it is best to stay still, other times this is not such a great idea. You need to learn about the temperament of each animal and react accordingly if you should come across any of them. Bears and mountain lions live in rural mountainous areas and hunt at night. So do not hike after dark or you could end up as dinner!

Bears do not like to be surprised, so let them know you are around by making a noise. A bear can weigh around 227 kg (500 lb), so do not let one get you in a bear hug, because you will never escape!

Black bears are very good at climbing trees, so do not try that as an escape route! If confronted by an angry bear, keep still. If the bear still attacks, hit back with anything you have. Strike its eyes or snout, which are its most vulnerable spots.

If faced by a stampeding bull, run to a safe spot (like the other side of a gate) fast! Otherwise, wave something to distract the bull. It is a myth that bulls are attracted to red; it is movement that attracts them. If the bull still charges, throw the object away from you and run.

Mountain lions are less likely to attack if you make yourself seem as big as possible. Stand still, open your coat wide and flap it around, and shout loudly! As a last resort, hurl objects at the lion to show you are not an easy target.

RULES TO REMEMBER

Avoid these situations at all costs:

Animals defending a fresh kill. ✶ **Females protecting their young.** ✶ Sleeping in the same clothes you cook in. ✶ **Leaving fresh food lying around.** ✶ Keeping food inside your tent. ✶ **Storing rubbish near your campsite.**

Things to remember

✶ Mountain lions often attack by jumping on prey from a high ledge and aiming at vulnerable areas, like the neck, so never curl up into a ball.

✶ Always back away slowly from a mountain lion or wait for it to walk away; running from the lion will only excite it.

Snakes in the grass

Snakes often have similar markings, so it can be difficult to tell a poisonous snake from a non-poisonous one. The best way to avoid getting bitten is to stay well away from all snakes. That means no prodding, poking, or swift movements, and no creeping closer to take a photograph. Never assume that a snake is dead because it is not moving. Some snakes only move to strike when prey is close!

Never try to suck out snake venom; if the poison gets in your mouth, it could enter your bloodstream.

If you are bitten by a snake, apply pressure to the wound and immobilize the affected part. Then wrap a bandage above the bite and bandage down over the wound. (See pages 46–47.)

If, for example, you have been bitten on the ankle, start bandaging at the knee. If possible, keep the affected area lower than the heart. This will slow the flow of the venom and give you valuable time to seek proper medical treatment.

Constrictors, like boas and pythons, do not use poisonous venom to attack their victim. Instead, they kill their prey by constriction, or squeezing them to death! To try and release a constrictor's grip, attempt to control its head and unwrap the coils.

If it is any consolation, most pythons will strike, then try to get away. Although they can quite easily swallow small children whole!

HOW TO PROTECT YOURSELF FROM SNAKES

• • • • • • • • • • • • • • • • • • • •

Wear thick leather boots. ✷ **Never corner a snake. Back off slowly and most snakes will slither away.** ✷ Check bedding, packs, and clothes before putting them on, as snakes may use them as a shelter. ✷ Keep to marked trails. ✷ Never put your hands or feet into places you cannot see.

Things to remember

✷ Never place ice on a snake bite; it makes it harder to remove the venom through a suction device.

✷ Do not tie bandages too tightly; you could cut off blood flow.

✷ Never try to "cut out" venom from a bite; this could cause an infection.

Sharks, bees, and alligators

What do you do if, while out swimming, you turn round, and find yourself staring into the big, beady eyes of a shark! Now your first reaction will probably be to swim away as fast as you can. But you will never out-swim a shark, so you are better off fighting back. But in the case of the Africanized Honeybee, or killer bee, your best bet is to cover your head and run for shelter at top speed! And as for alligators, well you had better read on and take note.

If you encounter a shark, it is probably just curious and will most likely swim away. But if it attacks, fight back! Use a camera, your fist, a rock, in fact anything that is hard, to smash the shark in the eyes or gills. It is a myth that a shark's nose is the most sensitive part of its body; the eyes and gills are more sensitive.

Most shark attacks happen in near-shore waters. But all marine waters are a potential risk, so always swim in groups and never at night.

If a bee stings you, remove the stinger immediately by raking your fingernail across it in a sideways motion.

Domesticated bees and wasps do not usually attack people unless they are angry. If a bee or wasp flies around you, run away, do not swat it, as that will make it angry and more likely to sting you.

Africanized Honeybees are the cousins of domestic bees. They form massive swarms and pursue their "enemies" for far greater distances than domesticated bees, making them very dangerous.

HOW TO AVOID BEE AND WASP STINGS

Keep your distance from swarms and colonies. ✱ Cover your head and run to a safe shelter. If no shelter is available, run through bushes, long grass, or weeds. ✱ Do not jump into water, as bees will wait for you to come up for air.

What do you do if an alligator attacks you? Try to cover its eyes to sedate it. If you are on land, leap onto its back, then push down hard on its neck to force the head and jaws down, so it cannot bite you.

If an alligator does trap you in its jaws, try to keep its jaws shut to prevent it from chewing or shaking you. A sharp tap on an alligator's nose usually makes it open its jaws, releasing anything it is holding.

Weather watch

It is difficult enough to survive outdoors without getting soaked in a thunderstorm or burned in the midday sun. If you learn the tips described here, you can predict weather changes and prepare yourself accordingly. Just by studying clouds, it is possible to predict strong winds, rain, fair weather, and fog. With the help of a protractor, you can measure wind speed and this may even help you to forecast approaching storms.

When outdoors, always wear plenty of high-factor sun cream, and re-apply it every two to three hours.

The shape, size, colour and texture of clouds will tell you if you are in for a wet weekend! High, small, white, lumpy clouds usually indicate fair weather. When a thin, hazy, grey or white sheet begins to thicken, rain may not be too far away. A low, sheet-like cloud that covers hills, produces fog. High clouds usually indicate good weather, low clouds bring rain.

Snow, sand, and water all reflect the sun's rays, so you need to wear clothes that will protect you from burning in these conditions. You may feel quite cool on a cloudy, windy day, but the sun's hot rays will still burn you.

Wind speed often indicates changes in the weather, so you need to keep an eye on what the wind is doing. Strong winds can cause sandstorms, rock falls, and even tidal waves. They can also be a sign of approaching tornadoes or hurricanes. (See pages 40–41 for more on strong winds and what to do if you are caught in one.)

MEASURING WIND SPEED WITH A PROTRACTOR

Wrap 50 cm (1.5 ft) of thread around the bar of a protractor. Secure the thread with a reef knot. (See page 9.) ✳ Tape the other end of the thread to a small rubber ball. ✳ Hold the protractor upside-down. When held parallel to the wind, you can read the angle the ball is blown to by the wind, and work out the wind speed. ✳

30° = 50 kph (30 mph) 60° = 25 kph (15 mph)
75° = 10 kph (6 mph) 90° = 0 kph (0 mph)

Things to remember

✳ Wear clothes made from tightly woven fabric and a sun hat that covers the back of your neck and ears, to protect you from the sun.

✳ Make sure you wear sunglasses that filter out all of the sun's harmful rays.

✳ To stop yourself from getting dehydrated on hot days, always drink plenty of water.

Safe swimming

Like most other things, you have to learn how to swim. Unless you have been swimming since you were a baby, you cannot leap into water and expect to be able to swim straight away. It takes time and patience. To learn how to swim, ask an adult to teach you, or better still, go along to your local swimming pool and take lessons from a qualified instructor. They will also teach you what to do in emergency situations, like how to float to conserve energy while waiting for rescue.

You must be a competent swimmer before going into the sea. Although the water may look calm, it can change in seconds, producing huge waves that can carry you out to sea or crash you against jutting rocks. Tidal water also has undertows. These are currents below the surface that pull you out to sea.

Although there may be fewer hazards to contend with in a swimming pool, you still need to keep within your limitations. That means, if you are not a strong swimmer, make sure that an adult is watching you at all times, and stay at the shallow end.

One of the worst things to get while you are swimming is cramp! Ooh, the pain! You can get cramp almost anywhere including your arms, legs, stomach, neck, hands, and feet.

If you get cramp while swimming, DO NOT PANIC! If you lose control and start swallowing water, you will drown! Tread water and breathe slowly. Call for help and wave one arm to attract attention.

EMERGENCY FLOATS

If you are out sailing and get swept overboard, remember the following:

Plastic bottles, large cans, and logs will help to keep you afloat until you are rescued. ✳ To make a float, put your clothes in a waterproof bag: leave plenty of air space. Tie the neck, bend it over, and tie it again. ✳ If you are with other people, split into groups of four. Tie your bags together; tied bags make a good support for someone who is injured or cannot swim.

Things to remember

✳ Always wait at least one hour after eating before you go swimming.

✳ If a warning flag or sign tells you it is not safe to swim, DO NOT swim.

Lost at Sea

What do you do if you are at sea and a huge wave damages your boat? Unless the boat is sinking, stay aboard and radio for help. If it is sinking, stay calm and prepare to board your lifeboat. Work as a team, each person responsible for a particular task. For example, one of you can ensure there is enough fresh water on the lifeboat, while another collects food. Try not to panic, this will only hinder your chances of survival.

 You should always be accompanied by an experienced sailor at sea.

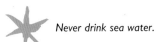 *Never drink sea water.*

Ocean waters move constantly, and how they move dictates the climate and living conditions for plants and animals. Sea currents are affected by the water's salinity (how salty it is), wind, and heat content. As sea currents are so unpredictable, there is always a danger of being swept away when you least expect it, so be prepared for any sudden changes.

If you do have to abandon ship, calmly put on a life jacket, and make your way to the lifeboat. You are more likely to die of exposure or hypothermia than anything else, so if you have time, collect warm clothing, including a hat and gloves.

Large ships have solid life boats, but smaller vessels have inflatable dinghies. If your dinghy is not self-inflating, it will have a pump that you can use to inflate it manually. Dinghies are made in sections, so there are several inflation points.

If you are in the water, board your dinghy at the end, never at the centre. Holding on to the dinghy, place one leg over the edge and roll into the vessel.

EMERGENCY SEA SURVIVAL KIT

Life jacket ✸ Warm clothes ✸ Torch (with extra batteries) ✸ Fresh drinking water in portable containers ✸ Tinned food, especially vegetables (they also contain drinking water), tin opener, chocolate, and boiled sweets ✸ Blankets ✸ VHF radio to call for help ✸ Hand-held flares to signal passing aircraft ✸ Compass and Global Positioning Satellite (GPS) unit to tell where you are.

Things to remember

✸ Few seabirds fly more than 160 km (100 miles) from land. They fly away from land before noon and towards it after noon.

✸ Continuous bird cries usually indicate land is not far away.

✸ A change in sea direction may be caused by the tide pattern around an island.

Surviving strong winds

Hurricanes and tornadoes are incredibly fast-moving, strong winds. Hurricanes have sustained winds of at least 119 km (74 miles) per hour. Do not be fooled by how cool they look on your TV screens. The big, brawny guy who drives straight through a hurricane and rescues the town is only acting! Every hurricane has an "eye" that can reach up to 483 km (300 miles) in width.

Hurricanes cause torrential rain, tornadoes, and flooding. Tornadoes are huge whirlwinds. They are probably even more dangerous than hurricanes if you receive a direct hit. The good news is they do not last as long.

Do not think the danger is over if a hurricane calms down for about half an hour, you are in the eye of the storm. Once the eye passes, the winds blow from the opposite direction, and anything that has been broken by the first winds hurtles through the air!

If you are inside when a hurricane or tornado approaches, go to a basement, a centre hallway, a bathroom, or toilet on the lowest floor. Make sure you keep clear of windows and any potential flying objects.

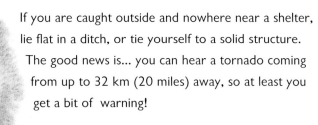

If you are caught outside and nowhere near a shelter, lie flat in a ditch, or tie yourself to a solid structure. The good news is... you can hear a tornado coming from up to 32 km (20 miles) away, so at least you get a bit of warning!

STRONG WIND EMERGENCY KIT

First aid kit ✷ Battery-powered torch and radio ✷ Extra batteries ✷ Warm, waterproof clothing and sleeping bags ✷ 14 litres of water (per person, per day) ✷ Tinned food and a tin opener ✷ Lidded bucket and toilet paper (come on, even the most hardened survivor will need to use the bucket after a few hours!)

Things to remember

- ✷ Listen to the local radio or TV station for instructions and advice.
- ✷ Never use a naked flame. Use a torch instead.
- ✷ Look out for fallen power lines.
- ✷ Stay clear of flooded areas.
- ✷ Never stay inside a car or mobile home.

Dangers above and below

If an **avalanche** or an earthquake starts and you do not know what to do, you may find yourself in serious trouble! So read on and take note. An avalanche usually occurs on slopes of 30°–45° within 24 hours of a snowfall. They are often caused by loud noises. So, after a major fall, always wait one day for the snow to settle. You do not get much warning before an earthquake. So, if you are in an earthquake area be prepared.

Avalanche danger areas are on the leeward side of mountains (the side facing away from the wind), snow-covered convex slopes, and deep snow-filled gullies. If buried by an avalanche, it is hard to escape. So lay flat and use the crawl swimming stroke to stay on top of the snow. Cover your nose and mouth to avoid swallowing snow.

If you are completely buried, try to dig a small hole around yourself and spit in it. The saliva should head downwards, giving you an idea of which direction is up. Use your hands, feet, a ski pole, or anything else you have, to push away the snow until you reach the surface.

If you live in or are visiting an earthquake area, make sure you have emergency supplies. They should include: food, torch (and spare batteries), radio (battery-operated), first-aid kit, fire extinguisher, blankets, and fresh clothing.

During an earthquake you need to think fast, be decisive, organized, and always prepared. Tune in to your local radio station for reports and advice, as this could save your life. What actions you take will depend on your situation; look in the box below.

WHERE TO GO DURING AN EARTHQUAKE

If you are at home, stay there! Find an inside corner, away from glass, and climb under a desk or table for added protection. A lower floor or basement is your best chance of survival.

If you are outside, stay away from buildings, power lines, and anything heavy that could fall. Do not go underground, in a tunnel, or in a lift. You could get trapped.

Things to remember

* Never ski alone in an avalanche area.
* Snow mobiles are fun and can be ridden high up in mountains, but they are also the main cause of avalanches.

Stormy weather

There is a saying that "lightning never strikes twice in the same place". Well it does! No place is one hundred percent safe from lightning, but some places, like high ground, are more dangerous than others. Large, enclosed buildings are generally much safer than smaller, open structures. But the risk of being struck by lightning also depends on what materials were used to construct the building and whether it has lightning protection.

During a storm, do not hold metal objects. Keep away from metal structures and fences, tall trees, hill brows, and large bodies of water; such as rivers, ponds, and oceans. Good places to shelter are in a car, or deep inside a large cave. Never shelter inside a cave mouth or under an overhang of rock.

If you are caught in a field or other open area, do not sit on anything that is waterlogged. Sit on something like a length of coiled rope. Then, bend your head down and hug your knees tightly to your chest, lifting your feet off the ground and drawing in your arms and legs.

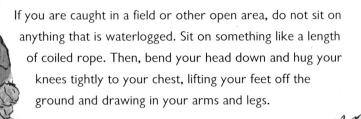

If you are inside, do not touch anything made of metal with exposure to outside; such as sinks, showers, metal doors and window frames. You could provide a contact to conduct the lightning, making you sizzle like a sausage!

The threat of lightning usually lessens with time after the last clap of thunder. But if a lightning storm is in your area, take care. Lightning can still exist even when there is a clear sky, no rain, and sunshine.

Things to remember

* During a lightning storm, unplug computers and any other electrical items that could be damaged by a surge of electricity.

* Stay inside if possible. If you are in a car, roll up the windows, and do not touch anything metal.

HOW FAR AWAY IS A LIGHTNING STORM?

When you see lightning flash across the sky, count the number of seconds until you hear thunder, and then divide by five. This will tell you how many miles the storm is from you. (Sound travels at 335 km [1,100 feet] per second.) If the time delay between seeing the lightning flash and hearing the thunder is less than thirty seconds, you should find a safer location immediately.

Slings and bandages

No matter how careful you try to be, there is always the possibility of an accident happening. Most minor injuries can be treated quickly and effectively, providing you have basic first aid knowledge. A couple of bandages, slings, and safety pins can go a long way to making you more comfortable if you have an accident, so always pack some in your first aid kit. If the injury is more serious, you will need to call the emergency services.

Sprain injuries can be painful, but they are nowhere near as serious as a broken bone! To treat sprains, bathe the affected area with cold water to reduce the swelling. Support the injury with a bandage, but do not restrict circulation. Elevate the affected limb and rest it completely.

BROKEN COLLARBONE OR ELBOW

You cannot set a broken collarbone or elbow in a plaster cast, but you can support it in a sling, as described on page 47. If you do not have a triangular sling, use a collar and cuff sling for a suspected collarbone or elbow fracture. Wrap a strip of material or tights around the wrist and tie the ends behind the neck.

MAKING A SLING

1 If an arm injury needs support and you do not have a sling or bandage, you can make one using a piece of material not less than 1 m (3 ft) square. This can be used to support and protect minor injuries to most body parts.

2 Fold the fabric diagonally to make a triangular bandage. Slip one end of the bandage under the arm and over the shoulder.

3 Bring the other end of the bandage over the other shoulder, cradling the arm. Tie the ends of the bandage behind the neck. A basic sling can also be used to protect the head, hand, chest, back, and feet.

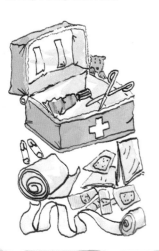

Things to remember

★ Always pack a first aid kit. It should contain triangular bandages, scissors, plasters, safety pins, gauze pads (for cleaning cuts and grazes), and antiseptic cream.

★ Keep your first aid kit in a waterproof bag or airtight container to keep it clean.

★ If you sprain your ankle, keep your boot on. It will act as a splint and support your ankle.

Stings and bites

Some stings and bites leave only small wounds, but can still be very dangerous, causing the victim to go into shock, and the heart to stop. They can cause blood poisoning, and in some cases, even death! An insect sting can cause severe allergic reactions, especially if there are multiple stings. Several stings from aggressive hornets could even be fatal. Mammals have very sharp teeth and may carry diseases, too.

If someone is bitten or stung, give the victim regular sips of water but NO food.

With bites from mammals, infection is the main risk. Make sure you are up-to-date with anti-tetanus shots. If you are travelling somewhere that rabies is a threat, remember to have a rabies vaccine before you leave.

Cleanse all bites for at least five minutes to remove the animal's saliva. Use a sterile, or at least very clean, non-fluffy material to bandage the wound. Never join bandages with knots, this can stop blood from circulating. Attach separate strips by binding over a previously applied layer.

Seek proper medical treatment to check a bite or sting as soon as possible.

Beware of stings and bites from spiders and scorpions, which inject powerful venom. Look out for creatures in undergrowth, inside tents and in bedding. Check clothing and shoes before putting them on.

If stung by a bee or wasp, immediately remove the stinger and venom sac by scraping a fingernail or blunt instrument across it in a sideways motion.

Never try to remove a stinger by pinching or plucking it. You will force more poison out of the stinger and into the victim's blood.

TREATING AN INSECT STING OR BITE

Make the victim comfortable, but do not move him. ✷ Apply pressure at the site of the wound and immobilize the affected part. ✷ Apply a bandage above the bite and bandage down over the bite. (See pages 46–47.)

Things to remember

✱ If the bite or sting is on an arm or leg, apply a splint to keep the limb straight.

✱ If the bite or sting is on the torso, apply pressure with a sterile, non-fluffy fabric.

✱ Centipedes have poison claws and strong jaws with poison fangs. Some tropical species are very dangerous to humans.

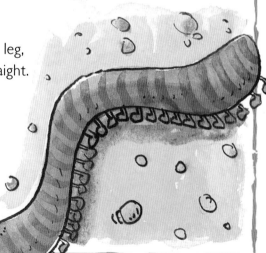

Cuts and grazes

Surviving in the wilderness is a tough business and could lead to a few scrapes. Cuts and grazes can easily become infected, so it is important to keep wounds clean and dry. If it is only a minor cut or graze, gently wash the affected area with warm, soapy water using a gauze pad or clean cloth. This will remove any dirt or gravel. Then, apply pressure to the injury with a clean non-fluffy pad to stop the bleeding, and cover the injury with a plaster.

Splinters are painful and can easily become infected if not removed quickly. To remove a splinter, thoroughly wash the affected area with warm, soapy water, making sure you do not push the splinter any further into the skin.

Use sterilized tweezers to grasp the splinter as close to the skin as possible. Pull out the splinter at the angle it went in. Gently squeeze the area around the wound to encourage a little bleeding. This will flush out any dirt. Wash the area again, pat it dry and cover with a waterproof plaster to keep it clean.

Cuts and grazes should also be washed and covered with a plaster. If a cut or graze is more serious, or covers a large area, it may be necessary to use a bandage to cover the wound. See pages 46–47 for information on bandaging.

If the cut is deep or large, or there is a lot of blood, you need to seek medical advice immediately. The patient may need stitches.

BUTTERFLY STITCHES

When your mother and father were kids, a needle and thread were used to stitch big cuts. Once the wound healed, the patient had to go back to hospital to have the stitches removed. Yuk. Thankfully, nowadays we have butterfly stitches and tape to seal most big cuts.

Things to remember

★ Gauze pads in first aid kits come in sealed paper wrappers to keep them clean and sterile, or germ-free.

★ Antiseptic wipes are handy for cleaning injured skin if you do not have clean water and soap available.

Blisters and sunburn

A **blister** on the heel of your foot can be agony and may hinder your progress considerably. Sunburn and heatstroke are another two things to watch out for. But if you take the proper precautions, you can minimize the chances of these things happening to you! Remember, the sun is at its hottest between 11 am and 1 pm, so avoid going out at these times, and always wear plenty of sunblock.

Wear comfortable walking boots that do not rub your heels, and thick cotton socks that come up over the top of your boots. Remember that the latest fashion footwear might look cool, but high-heeled sandals will not do a thing for your corns and bunions!

If a blister does appear, wash it with warm, soapy water and then rinse. Use a sterilized pad to pat the blister dry. Cover the blister with a plaster or non-fluffy dressing during the day. At night, leave it uncovered to let the air dry it out.

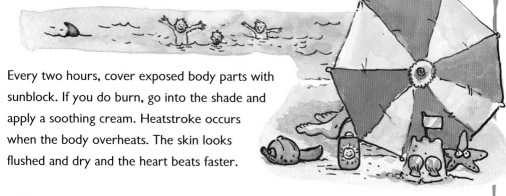

Every two hours, cover exposed body parts with sunblock. If you do burn, go into the shade and apply a soothing cream. Heatstroke occurs when the body overheats. The skin looks flushed and dry and the heart beats faster.

Always wear a hat that protects the back of your neck, as well as your head.

Someone with heatstroke may feel dizzy and hot, and get a headache. If this happens, lie her in the shade and remove all outer clothing. Sponge her with cool water until her temperature returns to normal.

SEEK MEDICAL ASSISTANCE IF

The skin blisters or bleeds. ✶ There are signs of faintness, dizziness, rapid pulse, rapid breathing, increased thirst, pale skin, clammy or cool skin. ✶ The eyes are painful and light sensitive. ✶ You feel nauseous, have a fever, chills or a rash. ✶ The sunburn is severe and painful.

Things to remember

✶ Sunburn can make you lose a lot of water, so drink at least six to eight glasses of water or fruit juice daily.

✶ Witch hazel, aloe vera, and camomile lotions all help ease sunburnt skin.

Being vigilant

Today, **more than ever,** you need to be vigilant at all times and aware of your surroundings. No matter what your age or size, if you do not behave sensibly and take proper precautions, there is always a chance you could be harmed. Here are a few rules to follow to help keep you safe on the streets. But do not spend all your waking hours worrying about what might go wrong, otherwise you will never have any fun.

✳ Always tell your parents or carers where you are going, which route you are taking, and when you will be home.

✳ If you are visiting someone, make sure your parents or carers know the person's name, address, and telephone number.

 Never use short cuts across deserted areas, such as wasteland, woodland, car parks, or underground walkways, even during daylight.

✳ Stay alert and aware of possible dangers, even when you are close to home.

✳ Never show off and take unnecessary risks to impress your friends!

Remember to charge your mobile phone regularly, make sure it is switched on, and take it with you whenever you go out. Store the phone numbers of other family members, just in case your parents are not at home and you need help.

If there is an emergency and you have to vacate a building or station, stay calm, listen to any announcements being made, and follow the instructions given. Do not panic, as this will only hinder your progress.

If you have to evacuate a building, never use the lift unless you are specifically told to do so. Use the stairs instead.

SUSPICIOUS PACKAGES

If you spot a bag or package that has been left unattended, DO NOT go near it – it may contain a bomb. ✳ If you are with an adult, tell him or her what you have seen. If not, report the suspicious package to someone in authority, such as a police officer or security guard. ✳ Leave the area as quickly and calmly as possible.

Things to remember

✳ Do not wear flashy jewellery or openly carry expensive items, like laptops or telephones, when you are out. They are just what muggers are looking for.

✳ Do not keep your wallet in your back pocket, or sling an open bag over your shoulders. This will make you an easy target for pickpockets. Instead, keep your wallet out of sight and your bag closed.

Street-smart

Knowing how to read train and bus maps and timetables are vital skills for urban survival. These skills will help you to find your way around, not only in an emergency but in everyday life, too. We have outlined the basics here.

TUBE TRAVEL

There are many routes or lines you can travel on on the underground. Each one is represented by a different-coloured line on the map.

You need to know three things: the name of the station you are travelling from, the station you want to reach, and the line that will take you there.

Not all journeys can be reached directly, so you may need to change lines at some point along the way.

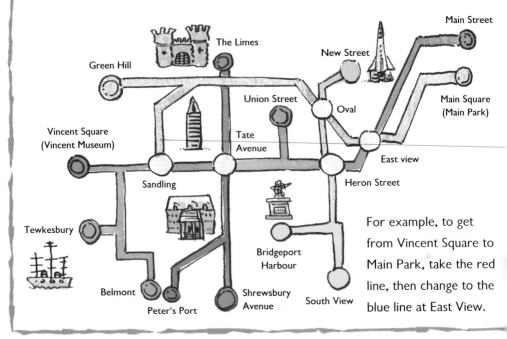

For example, to get from Vincent Square to Main Park, take the red line, then change to the blue line at East View.

BUS AND TRAIN TRAVEL

Bus and train timetables vary, but they all follow a similar principle. Each service is usually split into two halves, one for each direction, then divided into blocks, indicating the days of the week they run.

1 To use this bus timetable, look down the left-hand column and choose your starting point.

2 Trace across the page to find your required departure time. Check the top of this vertical column for any coded symbols and refer to the bottom of the page for their meaning.

VINCENT SQUARE – BRIDGEPORT HARBOUR   **42A**

Via Sandling, Peter's Port, Main Square

MONDAYS TO SATURDAYS

Operator	BT	BT	SC	SC	BT		SC	BT		BT
Service No:	244	244	44	44	244		44	244		244NS
Days		NS		S						
	am	am	am	am	am					pm
Vincent Square (Vincent Museum)	6.12	6.52	7.35	7.35	8.02		35	10		6.10
Sandling	....	6.56	7.39	7.39	8.06		39	14		6.14
Main Square (Main Park)	....	7.00	7.44	7.44	8.11		44	19		6.19
Peter's Port	6.17	7.04	7.50	7.50	8.17		50	25		6.25
Main Street (Main Crematorium)	6.21	7.09	7.54	7.54	8.21		54	29		6.29
Bridgeport Harbour	6.26	7.12	7.59	M	8.26		49	34		6.34

then at these mins past each hour ... *until*

NS:	Does not run on Saturdays
S:	Runs on Saturdays only
M:	Continues to Madison (arrives 9.02pm)
BT:	Operated by Blakes Travel
SC:	Operated by Styles Coaches

3 Read down the same column to find the destination arrival time. If there is no time against a place, this means the bus does not stop at that point.

Stranger danger

Does it get on your nerves when your parents keep repeating themselves over and over again! Well, we know you have probably heard all this before, but some things really are worth repeating and listening to! After all, the last thing you want to hear when you have ignored good advice is, "We told you so!" So, at the risk of being called fuddy-duddies, here are a few tips on what to do, and not do, when out in the big, wide world!

If you get lost in a crowd or a shopping centre, look for someone in uniform, like a police officer, fire officer, or security guard, or go into a shop and speak to a sales assistant. Explain what has happened and ask them to phone your parents or carers to tell them where you are.

STRANGER DANGER

Unless a parent or carer has told you that it is safe to do so, NEVER go off with someone you do not know, for any reason! If a stranger approaches you, immediately tell your parent, carer, or someone in authority what has happened and describe what the stranger looked like.

Imagine you are out on your own, and you have somehow managed to take the wrong train, or maybe the vehicle you are travelling in has been diverted. You know your regular route off by heart, but now you are completely lost and have no clue how to get home!

What do you do? Do not panic or start crying as you leap up and down, waving your arms in the air. That really won't help!

Never approach a stranger in the hope that they might take you home. And do not start walking aimlessly, thinking you might recognize somewhere familiar.

Ask the driver or a police officer to put you on a bus or train that will take you to your correct destination. If you have a mobile phone, call home to say what has happened.

Things to remember

* If a stranger approaches you, say very loudly, "I don't know you. Please go away."
* If you have a mobile phone, keep it charged, and always take it with you whenever you go out.
* Try to travel with someone else, so you are not on your own if you do get lost.

Coping with a fire

Fires can start for all kinds of reasons, and quickly rage out of control. If a fire does start near you, leave the area immediately. Never try to put out the fire, as you could get severely burnt. Call the emergency services, and ask for the fire department. In a clear voice give your name and the address where the fire is burning. Do not hang up until the operator tells you it is okay to do so, just in case he or she has any other important questions to ask you.

Most fires that begin at home are caused by chip pans overheating on the cooker and cigarettes left unattended. Whatever the cause, if a fire starts, alert anyone else in the house, and evacuate immediately! Tell an adult which room the fire is in, and let him or her deal with it.

The only warning you may get if there is a fire in your home is the sound of a fire alarm going off; especially if you are asleep! So if you do not have a fire alarm fitted already, nag your parents until they have one installed. IT COULD SAVE YOUR LIFE!

If you are inside when a fire starts, stop what you are doing, drop to the floor, and crawl out below the smoke. Recite this phrase to help you remember what to do "Stop. Drop. Crawl."

 Water and electricity do not mix. Never throw water onto an electrical fire.

If you are trapped inside a building when a fire starts and there is no escape route, follow the instructions in the box below.

IF YOU ARE TRAPPED IN A BUILDING

Close any doors between you and the fire. Put bedding or towels along the bottom of the door to seal the gap. ✱ Call the fire service. Give the address, the floor you are on, and exactly where you are on that floor. ✱ Open the window and stay near it for fresh air and to let the firefighters see you. ✱ If there is no window, cover your face with a wet cloth to help prevent smoke fumes penetrating your lungs. Lie flat on the ground until help arrives.

Things to remember

✱ More people are killed or seriously injured by smoke from fires than the actual fires themselves.

✱ If a chip pan does ignite, an adult can throw a damp tea towel over it to put the fire out.

Mechanical failure

You see it every day – cars, buses, and even trains that have broken down. It usually happens at the most inconvenient spot for everyone else trying to use that route! And, of course, it is always when you are in a rush. But spare a thought for the poor driver and passengers, because one day it might be your vehicle that has decided it does not want to go any further!

If you are travelling on a busy road, and the car you are in breaks down, DO NOT climb out, as you could easily be injured by passing traffic. Wait for the driver to tell you what to do. It might be safer to stay put until the car has been repaired.

If the car you are in has broken down in a dangerous spot where it could be hit by other vehicles, you may have to leave the vehicle and find a safe place to wait.

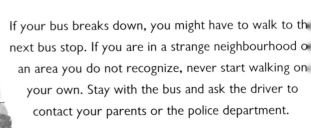

If your bus breaks down, you might have to walk to the next bus stop. If you are in a strange neighbourhood or an area you do not recognize, never start walking on your own. Stay with the bus and ask the driver to contact your parents or the police department.

Leaving a train that has broken down is a definite no-no! Over- and underground trains run on live tracks that are powered by electricity. If you accidentally step on one of these tracks, you will be electrocuted!

Wait for the train driver to give you instructions about what to do next. This may mean staying where you are and waiting for the train to be repaired or waiting for the fire service. Do not get off the train unless told to do so.

IF YOU GET STUCK IN A LIFT

Press the alarm button. ✶ If there is a telephone, call the operator and say how many people are stuck in the lift. ✶ If you know which floors you are stuck between, tell the operator. ✶ If there is enough room, sit down and relax until help arrives.

Things to remember

✶ If you are travelling by car in a rural area, ensure the driver has checked there is enough petrol in the car. Or you may have a long walk if you run out of petrol!

✶ If the breakdown delays your journey, call ahead to let people at your destination know you are going to be late and why.

Useful contacts

Name _____

Address _____

_____

Telephone: home _____

mobile _____

Emergency services _____

Police station _____

Fire station _____

Mum's mobile phone _____

Dad's mobile phone _____

Mum's work _____

Dad's work _____

Doctor's surgery _____

Local hospital _____

Dentist's surgery _____

School _____

Gas company _____

Electric company _____

Plumber _____

Friend _____

Friend _____

Friend _____

Other useful contacts: